The Inclusive
Republic of Australia

A Climate Change Champion

by Rod Williams

First published by Limelight Publishing 2022
Copyright © 2022 Rod Williams
All Rights Reserved.
ISBN (p): 978-1-4709-3269-5
ISBN (e): 978-1-4716-0104-0

Cover design: Limelight Publishing
Layout and typesetting: Limelight Publishing
Editing: Meg Hellyer and Alexandra Williams
Cover photo: Angus Strachan, Teacher Extraordinaire-Ramingining NT

Limelight Publishing
PO Box 65, Narangba
Brisbane, Queensland Australia 4504

Lulu Press
PO Box 12018, Durham,
NC 27709 United States

lulu.com/spotlight/rpw
limelightpublishing.com
lulu.com

Contents

About the Author

Rod Williams was born in Australia and spent his childhood in the playground of Manly Beach, Sydney. The beach was his daycare centre. Rugby and surf boat rowing became his sports. He was born with itchy feet to travel.

In 1978, after completing his commerce studies, he left home to see the world at age twenty-three. His first overseas trip saw him catch the Trans-Siberian railroad across Russia which excited him for more adventure. He had departed Australia with only a duffle bag and returned eighteen years later with a 40ft container, his wife, Sheila, and their four daughters. Two born in the USA, one in Switzerland and one in London.

In those overseas years, he lived and worked in Oakland California, Verbier Switzerland, London, Paris and Newburyport Massachusetts.

Rod has travelled in over seventy countries and conducted business in forty during his business development career. He has always had a keen interest in history and what makes people tick in each of those societies. He jokingly says he has a PHD in Life Experience.

He now lives in Santa Cruz California with his wife Sheila and youngest daughter, Sophie, returning to Australia in 2024. He considers himself bi-coastal, but in his case, meaning West Coast USA and East Coast Australia. He is still a keen skier, mountain biker and rower.

I would like to thank all the traditional owners for their patience and for maintaining hope. My hope is that you can get a better deal from your fellow Australians.

It's time

- To embrace our First Nations peoples, to see them, to hear them, to give them a voice, to acknowledge our history with them, to include them in our national vision of the future and to begin the healing.

- Then to become an Independent Republic.

- To get back in rhythm with the planet, to get back in balance with our ecosystem, to show more respect to the animal kingdom.

- To recognise and accept our responsibility and role in the fight against climate change.

Let us Australians use this pivotal time to show the world a bold, independent Australia, reconciled with and proud of its First Nations peoples and the courage to change.

Uluru Statement from the Heart

As read out at the 2017 First Nations National Constitutional Convention at Uluru

We, gathered at the 2017 National Constitutional Convention, coming from all points of the southern sky, make this statement from the heart:

Our Aboriginal and Torres Strait Islander tribes were the first sovereign Nations of the Australian continent and its adjacent islands, and possessed it under our own laws and customs. This our ancestors did, according to the reckoning of our culture, from the Creation, according to the common law from 'time immemorial', and according to science more than 60,000 years ago.

This sovereignty is *a spiritual notion*: the ancestral tie between the land, or 'mother nature', and the Aboriginal and Torres Strait Islander peoples who were born therefrom, remain attached thereto, and must one day return thither to be united with our ancestors. This link is the basis of the ownership of the soil, or better, of sovereignty. It has never been ceded or extinguished, and co-exists with the sovereignty of the Crown.

How could it be otherwise? That peoples possessed a land for sixty millennia and this sacred link disappears from world history in merely the last two hundred years?

With substantive constitutional change and structural reform, we believe this ancient sovereignty can shine through as a fuller expression of Australia's nationhood.

Proportionally, we are the most incarcerated people on the planet. We are not an innately criminal people. Our children are aliened from their families at unprecedented rates. This cannot be because we have no love for them. And our youth languish in detention in obscene numbers. They should be our hope for the future.

These dimensions of our crisis tell plainly the structural nature of our problem. This is *the torment of our powerlessness*.

We seek constitutional reforms to empower our people and take *a rightful place* in our own country. When we have power over our destiny our children will flourish. They will walk in two worlds and their culture will be a gift to their country.

We call for the establishment of a First Nations Voice enshrined in the Constitution.

Makarrata is the culmination of our agenda: *the coming together after a struggle.* It captures our aspirations for a fair and truthful relationship with the people of Australia and a better future for our children based on justice and self-determination.

We seek a Makarrata Commission to supervise a process of agreement-making between governments and First Nations and truth-telling about our history.

In 1967 we were counted, in 2017 we seek to be heard. We leave base camp and start our trek across this vast country. We invite you to walk with us in a movement of the Australian people for a better future.

Introduction

I decided to write this book, complete with my own personal 'Dreaming' (white fella's version), simply because I believe with all my heart and soul that there is no better time for Australia to come of age and become an independent, proud republic than now.

To go forward with our own unique character, we must first recognise the spiritual bond between our Indigenous people and the land they never surrendered. To tell the truth of our violent history with them and in this process attempt true recognition and reconciliation. To strive for a genuine, broad-based understanding of our First Nations peoples and their cultures. The days of ignoring and erasing the dark chapters should end. Transparency is long overdue. Dare we learn, and dare we remember.

Let's walk forward together as one with a common vision of our nation's future, proud of our 60,000 years of history – not only the 250 years since white man's arrival.

Australia is indeed a lucky country, as it has been called many times, largely thanks to a small population who've shared a large portion of bountiful natural resources. Our 7.6 million square kilometers, 25.8 million people and 25,760 kilometres of coastline is inhabited today by a cosmopolitan, multinational population of educated, resilient and innovative people.

I have lived in Europe, UK, and currently reside in the USA. During the last forty years, I have traveled and worked in fifty plus countries, and I can assure you that Australia is really a very, very good country, providing a fine lifestyle for most of its citizens. We are not perfect, but we are better than many. I would say better than most.

Can we do better? Absolutely.

Have there been mistakes made? Yes.

Is there inequality? Yes.

Is there racism and white privilege? Yes.

Healing is needed in ever-increasing ways and on many levels of our being, individually and collectively. We need to heal our relationship with both our First Nations peoples and Mother Nature. Our indigenous people can help us heal our relationship with the natural world. They lived and prospered here for 60,000 years before colonialism with a very light footprint.

We have the personal freedom, the national wealth and the skills to challenge the status quo, to help others and to self-improve in the process. The question is – do we believe we can do better and, if so, do we accept the challenge?

We need strong leadership that will have the courage to acknowledge our history, begin the healing and excite us to strive for our future together. To challenge us to achieve a satisfying and more sustainable life, not just for ourselves, but for the wider community as well. We should be proud of where we are going as a nation and feel we are all part of an inclusive team on a united noble journey.

Australia, like the world in general, seems bereft of true statesmen or stateswomen – nation builders who think and act more nobly for the common good, and not just for their own career promotion or paid self interest groups. Is it time for baby boomer politicians to stand aside and allow the next generations to take the reins? Time for some new visionary energetic leadership for our country.

A Climate Change Champion

As a developed, wealthy nation with highly educated people, let us accept our international role and shared responsibility to address the global life-threatening and economy-destroying climate crisis. It must be addressed with a war-time urgency.

Our environment is changing dramatically and becoming less accommodating to both humans and the animal kingdom at an alarming pace. This degradation will continue to be a violent process, with more floods, more bushfires and extreme temperatures. Today the developed world struggles to assimilate a few million political refugees – just imagine a billion or more climate-displaced people.

We stand by while carbon dioxide and methane are pumped into the atmosphere, our forests are cut down and our oceans suffer through uncontrolled commercial overfishing (both legal

and illegal), agricultural pesticide and fertiliser run-off into
waterways and microplastics get into our food chain, all at
accelerating rates. This degradation of our forests and oceans
continues at a time when we need these biosystems to absorb
even more carbon dioxide-double jeopardy.

We Australians are part of the problem and we must become
an active part of the solution. Let's take a stand to protect from
further damage the truly wonderful ecosystem we all share and
help ensure its survival and regeneration. Let's leave our children,
grandchildren and great grandchildren a united country, a better
world, with an environment repairing and improving. We need to
plan for such an outcome, make structural changes and get
moving. The clock is ticking. The ticking is getting louder and
faster. We need strong leadership and an agreed national
direction with citizen buy-in and so willing participation. This is a
global challenge. Australia should be a leader, not a laggard.

With our environment under threat and dramatic behavioural
changes needed to avoid a calamity of epic proportions, is it not
an opportune time to take a good look at ourselves? Perhaps we
should re-examine how we want to participate in the global
community and what role we will play. This is a time for all hands
to the pumps, so let's enlist the skills and experience of our First
Nations peoples to repair our environment and to strengthen our
ties to it.

A Global Citizen

My firm belief is that the 21st century can be Australia's century. We can take great strides towards an even better quality of life for all our citizens, where we not only reach our full potential as a nation, but as an independent united nation, charting our own course and destiny. Let us stand tall and proud as a unique republic with our own declared principles and values. Let us then act as leading contributors to a massive global effort to fix our planet.

To labour a point, should this current perfect storm of global challenges be our catalyst to raise the bar and become a better global citizen, to be more environmentally accountable and more inclusive at home? I certainly believe so, and hope that many of my fellow Australians agree – for in doing so, we would progress to the next stage of our development as a proud, fair-minded nation and people. Maybe I am a dreamer, but what the hell. Dreaming might just be one of the learnings we can all embrace, inspired by our First Nations peoples.

I do not want to sugar-coat the massive task ahead. In the nearly 200 years since the dawn of the industrial revolution, economies have grown massively and tremendous wealth has been created, which mostly resides unfairly in the G20 countries, including our own. It has been a period of incredible invention, innovation, science, hard work and entrepreneurship. Sadly, it's also been a time of crushing Indigenous peoples, their cultures, taking their land and abusing Mother Nature. In Australia we had frontier wars with our First Nations peoples. There was genocide, massacres and torture. It's time to accept these harsh facts, to educate ourselves fully and truthfully, to recognise the stolen land, the abuse. It's time to give our First Nations peoples a real voice.

Economic progress has generated massive wealth and concentrated it in too few hands through the lack of true accountability in the modern industrial and agricultural processes. By this I mean historically, and still today, goods and services are costed typically by the material, labour, rent, overhead, freight etc. – the obvious and tangible costs. There is never a charge added for the very real (and ever growing) pollution to the public assets of air, land and water. Ironically if these costs had been levied, the realised profits would have been reduced, encouraging more innovation and engineering to reduce the polluting outputs and so raise corporate profits. History proves self-serving motivation is very reliable.

I am sure many exploited people would say the labour costs were a long way from fair as well. The bottom line is that the beneficiaries of this Industrial Age-created wealth must now pick up a lion's share of the tab to be fair, in order to correct environmental mistakes and abuses of the past.

In reality we will all need to make some sacrifices to pass on a better world to future generations. Baby boomers, of which I am one, have had a dream run of economic prosperity and should not pass the bulk of the burden onto future generations. The time for action is now, not down the road.

As citizens, we cannot just wait for government policy to change as a convenient reason for non-action. We must force the politicians to change the agenda. We must all get vocal and be willing to change. Empathetic government policy (both domestically and internationally) will be needed to make sure the burden does not fall too heavily on those least capable to pay.

Let's not be remembered as the generations that had the knowledge to understand the challenges and the means to fix them, but stood by whilst our First Nations peoples continued to struggle, our ecosystem and animal kingdom collapsed.

There are no excuses for inaction. I am personally so exhausted by the constant bad news that fills the airways and social media. To see and feel positive change and experience some tangible good news would be so uplifting. Real hope for a healed, united, honest Australia and a more equitable, sustainable world would be such a gift.

Chapter 1

A Brief History

Let's reflect for a moment on some key milestones and events in our country's history that have helped to shape the Australia of today.

For 60,000+ years, prior to the British colonialisation of the 18th century, our First Nations peoples had been calling this island, this continent, their home. Estimates put their number at anywhere from 500,000 up to one million.

These Indigenous peoples were spread across the entire continent. They were many and varied mobs speaking hundreds of languages. They had learned to live, survive and thrive in this land without any input from foreigners. They were farmers, fishermen and hunters. They trod lightly and ate sustainably, adapting to the land and native vegetation. They were mindful – they still are. They shared – they still do. They were self-sufficient.

They had their own law and didn't need anybody else's.

They never surrendered the land or gave away their sovereignty.

Their existence was first noticed by European explorers in the 17th and 18th centuries. Willem Janszoon, Luis Vaz de Torres,

Pieter Nuyts and Abel Tasman all visited and charted parts of the Australian coast, but the first explorer of real consequence to the First Nations peoples was the Brit James Cook.

The First Fleet

In 1770 Captain Cook sailed around Australia, anchoring in a few spots for fresh water, game, a little sightseeing and some random flag-planting which, from the British standpoint, made him an expert on all things Australian. Cook admitted in his diary that he actually shot an Aboriginal man from his dingy before even setting foot in Australia. Cook claimed he was trying to hurt him, not kill him. The victim's companions carried him back into the bush. His fate is unknown. This was probably not the best way to build working relationships.

On returning to Britain, empowered by his newly found 'in-depth knowledge', Cook declared the discovered land Terra Nullius, meaning 'a land without people.' (I think he meant 'without white people'). Admittedly this was a time before satellite images and drones, but he never ventured into the heartland (probably staying in sight of his ship at all times) to understand the folly of this statement. With a little exploration and an open mind, he would have observed that there were indeed people living harmoniously on and with the land – many people. I suspect Cook was politically savvy enough to tell the powers that be in London what they wanted to hear, particularly if he hoped to be commissioned for future adventures.

If the First Nations peoples had known of Cook's declaration, I am quite sure they would have disagreed. It was under this rather convenient pretense that Governor Phillip arrived with the First Fleet in 1788 to cement the British claim before other European powers did the same. The Fleet brought eleven ships to Australia, carrying 1,400 people, of which 750 were convicts.

(For full disclosure, my own heritage can be traced back to this fleet. My great, great, great grandmother was transported to the 'colony' aboard this First Fleet, which departed England in 1787. On arrival in Sydney, she gave birth to the first child in the new settlement. That baby was named Rebecca Small.)

With the American colonies rather inconveniently rallying together and declaring Independence, the British government had been forced to find a new destination for their surplus convicts. Where better than this far away unclaimed land.

In reality, Phillip's fleet was an invasion force. This aggressor status was legally confirmed by The Australian High Court's game-changing decision in the 1992 Mabo land case. The judges recognised that native title had existed for all Indigenous peoples long before the British occupation. During the next century, more and more British settlements were established. Not once was a treaty offered, negotiated or agreed with the Indigenous peoples. Maybe the prize was seen as too valuable.

When you consider the track record of colonialists in other countries where treaties were indeed signed, I am not convinced a treaty would have made a great deal of difference to the plight of our Indigenous communities. It must have been painfully obvious to the settlers as they moved inland that the country was in fact inhabited and farmed, and that they were invaders. There would have been ample evidence all around them.

Genocide

Due to this proliferation of the colonies and the continual push for more land, the 1800s became a century of oppression and frontier wars, with tens of thousands of Indigenous peoples killed and many more imprisoned. There were massacres as well as deliberate genocide. Aboriginal heroes stood tall in their homelands and tried to resist the powerful tide of oppression, but many were ultimately killed. Pemulwuy was shot and beheaded, and Musquito was hung.

The Indigenous people were treated like animals that had to be hunted and driven off the land. European diseases like smallpox, syphilis, and influenza were introduced both accidentally and deliberately, with devastating effects.

There was no attempt to understand the Indigenous ways or cultures. An attitude of white superiority was deeply entrenched. Many would say this is still true today. Land management techniques learned over thousands of years were simply ignored as vast tracks of land were cleared to make way for European farming practices, with both sheep and cattle introduced. Top soil was washed into the rivers, choking them.

Just as the USA had sustained ancient grasslands for massive herds of buffalo to graze on, Australia had millions of kangaroos living in our wonderful native grasslands.

The Gold Rush

The 1850s saw the Gold Rush, which brought great economic wealth to the nation whilst introducing new immigrants from China with a sprinkling of Americans, chasing a similar wealth to that of their own California gold rush. Again, disease was spread to Indigenous communities. Most notable of these diseases was smallpox, which was sometimes deliberately impregnated in gift blankets by the British soldiers. Even today, some Indigenous peoples in Arnhem Land will not eat wild horse meat despite being readily available, as historically it had been poisoned and given to them by stockmen.

Australian Federation

In 1901, at the dawn of the 20th century, the six British colonies were joined together and with the King's blessing, the Australian Federation was declared. The six colonies became states. Our First Nations peoples were never considered in the process. Legally they were invisible. Morally they were ignored. Physically they were abused, and their humanit denied.

The British Monarch remained the Head of State under the newly written Australian Constitution. The Monarch would then appoint a Governor-General to be the royal representative. Since the role's inception, in reality it has been a ceremonial role, with one big exception – when in 1975 the Governor-General John Kerr dissolved Gough Whitlam's elected Labor Government of the day and forced an election. It is still a point of debate as to whether his action was legal. The Australian people had chosen a government, and with her embedded constitutional powers, the Queen removed it.

It took this new Australian Federation until 1962 to grant the Indigenous population the right to vote, even while the Government continued a campaign to remove Indigenous children from their homes. This forced assimilation program started in 1910 in an effort to dilute the Aboriginal races into non-existence. Finally, it was halted in 1970, thereby putting an end to the infamous Stolen Generations.

There were Aboriginal Australians who tried to help the plight of their fellow Indigenous peoples – such as William Ferguson, who launched a civil rights campaign by founding The Aboriginal Progressive Association in 1937 – but these brave souls swam against a strong, ignorant white tide.

In the hope of gaining recognition as equals, the First Nations peoples made a number of direct appeals to the British Monarch, even volunteering for the Boer War and both World Wars. If you want to understand a true Indigenous Australian hero with incredible resilience, read about Cecil Ramalli. I know his story as he was an old boy of Hurlstone Agricultural High School, as am I. He had an Indian father and an Aboriginal mother. In 1938 he was picked, in his first year out of school, as the first Aboriginal to play for the Wallabies against the All Blacks. He went on to tour Britain with the 1939 Wallabies. On arrival in Britain, with war declared, the tour was canceled. On return to Australia, he signed up to join the army. He was captured with the fall of Singapore and worked on the infamous Thai Burma railroad. He survived that hell and was then transferred aboard a prison ship to Nagasaki to work in an underground coal mine. He was underground when the atomic bomb went off and so survived! What a hero— to be picked for the Wallabies, and then survive the war!

My dad fought the Japanese in New Guinea and came home at half his weight, so from his stories I can really appreciate Ramalli's story.

World War and Refugees

Following WW2, our population started to change and diversify. Immigration from Europe accelerated, with many displaced people looking for somewhere safe and the opportunity to start again.

This situation is not unlike the Iraqis, Syrians, and Afghans of today. Greeks, Italians, Brits, and even Germans, came to Australia, bringing their culture and cuisine with them. Australia needed the workers, as we had lost tens of thousands of men to the war.

One fine example of how this worked for both the refugees and Australia was the building of the Snowy Mountains Hydro-Electric Scheme, starting in 1949. This was a win/win project where we provided a new safe home for refugees and, in return, they built a hydro-electric power system, a massive piece of national infrastructure. It was designed to provide atomic bomb-proof electric power 'out of harm's way', and still contributes green energy to our society today. It was ahead of its time!

Multiculturism

Then, following the Vietnam War in the 1970s, we accepted many Vietnamese boat people, providing more diversity for us as a nation. Following on into the 1990s and to today, we have accepted refugees from Africa, Middle East, and Asia.

We could have been more compassionate and more generous for sure, but once again we admitted more diversity into our society. In total, Australia has accepted close to 10 million immigrants from many countries, of which only 160 thousand were British convicts. With our birth rate hovering just below two children per couple, we still depend today on immigration for

population growth. This immigration melting pot has given us the
multiculturalism we enjoy today.

The First Nations peoples could say they were multicultural
before the white man arrived, with their many languages, dialects,
food types and customs. They have a strong argument.

So, today, let's be super multicultural. We just need to
recognise and embrace all these roots, old and new. Our history
exists, good, bad and ugly. It cannot be undone. We must stop
filtering it. Let's acknowledge it, learn from it and move forward as
one.

As a society, I feel it is fair to say that we have definitely
moved on from a dominant white racist culture as evidenced by
the earlier 'White Australia' immigration policy, to a society that is
very diverse and more inclusive. Clearly, there is a long way to go
with the inclusiveness for our First Nations peoples, but there has
indeed been some progress. Change and assimilation takes time.
Listening and learning from each other takes time. Indeed, so does
learning to listen to each other. Let's work harder together.

We have learned to accept elements of the imported
immigrant cultures over time. Why have we spent less energy
understanding our Indigenous cultures, which grew from the land
we all call home? Why have we not been more curious and open
to sharing knowledge, broadening our culture? Why has the
European grass always been greener?

Time to Move On

I understand the historical British tie runs deep within our white Anglo population, and we would not be the country we are today without their contribution, both good and bad.

To ease any discomfort at cutting the ties, we should remember that after our military and political support, we were dropped by Britain as a preferred trading partner when the UK joined the EU in 1973. The British decided at the time that their future should be more tied to Europe than to their earlier colonies. This decision was understandable and logical following Europe's extreme makeover following WW2. This reasoning, however, does not alter the fact that we were pushed out into the cold. A large trading market was decimated overnight.

Maybe it is time we also put this colonial past behind us, just as the British did. Let us recognise this chapter of our history, but it should not define us. At the end of the day, it's only 250 years out of 60,000!

Chapter 2

Australia Today

Let's take stock of where we are today and what we have built as
a nation. Indulge me. You can agree or disagree, add or subtract,
but this is what I see:

OUR STRENGTHS

- A functioning democracy protecting our personal
  freedom. I look forward to adding 'independent' to
  'democracy'. As a nation, I think the majority of us take
  our personal freedom for granted. Can you imagine living
  in a state where you are awoken by a knock on your front
  door in the middle of the night, and a family member is
  dragged off, maybe to never been seen again? Even the
  possibility is so foreign to most of us. However, ask our
  Indigenous peoples, who are still dying in custody. They
  may question our application of personal freedom.

- The land itself, whether you believe it is a gift or a stolen
  bounty, with its many natural resources. Our country has
  paid a lot of bills by riding on the sheep's back, harvesting
  massive amounts of grains, and our world-leading miners
  digging up and selling rocks.

- A free, healthy lifestyle with real opportunity. A balanced lifestyle between family, work and play. Both Australia and New Zealand have a lifestyle many countries dream about. Our Australian summer family holidays at the beach or in the bush are such a cultural institution. They should be treasured for the wonderful tradition and gift they are for us all.

- A multicultural society. About a quarter of today's Australians were born overseas and 50% have at least one parent born overseas. I grew up in the 1960s on a diet of lamb chops, sausages, potatoes and peas, washed down with milk. I still don't like peas! Compare that diet to the gastronomic delights readily available in our modern society, thanks in great part to our various immigrant populations.

- A robust world-leading economy. It provides a high income per capita – $56,700 per person. Our economy is one of the best in the world.

- A world-class public education system.

- Affordable high-quality medical and disability care. I can tell you how wonderful Medicare is, having lived in the tragic USA health care system that provides care based on the level of your wealth. To me, the whole concept of NDIS is so Australian – mates helping mates.

- Incredibly beautiful, clean and functioning cities and towns. So many of the world's other great cities are nowhere near as clean or safe as Australia's capital cities.
- Skilled workforce including our world class farmers who battle floods, bushfires, droughts, politicians, and still deliver. Climate change is, and will, present them with bigger challenges. As part of this, maybe it's time to better understand, explore and embrace Indigenous sustainable practices.
- Our geographic location in Asia and on the Pacific rim. We are now in the centre of the action. Markets galore!

OUR WEAKNESSES

- True knowledge and full recognition of our Indigenous peoples and their culture, history, knowledge, skills and spiritual heritage. Importantly, their way of thinking. No other nation on earth can claim sixty thousand years of history.
- Reduced opportunity for our Indigenous peoples. They are still way behind white Australians with regards to family wealth and assets, which makes it harder for children to reach their full potential. In a practical sense, this makes borrowing to start a business very hard. White privilege still exists. Much of the time, the lucky white recipients do not even realise their advantage. Selfishly this means we

waste a national asset by not understanding their knowledge or realising their potential.

- Lack of recognition and acceptance of our role in global environmental issues, both their causes and solutions. Being a dry island continent with many coastal dwellers, climate change and ocean destruction should be of vital importance to the populace and engrained in government policymaking.

- Our small population with its relevant buying power. We will always need access to international markets to buy and sell.

- Recent political leadership has been ordinary at best, devoid of long-term vision and aspirations for our nation. At times, politicians remind me of spoiled trust fund kids who have inherited the wealth of previous generations, but somehow think it was all their doing. At the same time, they blame everybody else for any mistake or setback. Nor are they brave enough to ever be the first mover. Maybe our new government will do better. I hope so.

OUR OPPORTUNITIES

- To learn from our Indigenous peoples with their thousands of years of knowledge of our ecosystem, their traditional medicines, land management techniques, and

local foods; importantly, their way of thinking and
processing of issues and challenges. We all need to tread
more lightly, so all knowledge should be welcome. Our
First Nations peoples can be agents of change.

- Join the global effort to fight climate change. Really join.
  We can be a green energy superstar. New industries and
  jobs will be created. When all the world polluters finally
  embrace carbon taxes (China just has), the race to kill off
  carbon extraction industries and replace them with green
  power will really take off. At the same time, if the same
  governments have the courage to drop coal, oil and gas
  industry subsidies it will be a total game changer. Public
  opinion will eventually force this as climate chaos
  becomes more destructive and more personal. Let us be
  ready and competitive, and hope it is not too late. What a
  shame that we walked away from the Emissions Trading
  Scheme that the Gillard Labor Government launched in
  2011. We went from being a leader in addressing climate
  change to a laggard, with a single piece of backward
  legislation. The Liberal leadership chose to make it a
  political football, rather than a way to build a better more
  competitive future for our nation. Why not bring these
  carbon taxes back? The capital raised could be used as
  investment for new ventures and technologies advancing
  green climate solutions. For example, even now, we

should accelerate the development and rollout of Green Hydrogen and build the processing factories locally.

- We have abundant green resources of sun, tide, wind and uranium – yes, uranium. Today, the world needs nuclear power – both small modular reactor plants and large baseload plants – to buy us all time whilst we switch away from fossil fuels to solar, wind and other renewables. In early 2022, China commissioned one modular plant, with 150 more to follow. Backed by the UK government, Rolls Royce is currently working on a new reactor design. Let us join such an effort to design a generic nuclear plant that can be mass produced in a factory. We must shake off our fear of nuclear power, as in reality it is the only option today to get us through the hump in the next few decades. So why not build them for us and our Asian neighbours?

- The other less-talked-about global challenge, and another real opportunity for Australia, is the removal of the approximately one trillion tons of carbon dioxide already in the atmosphere. Simply put, it needs to be returned to our plants and soils. This will require new thinking, and challenge many of our current land uses, but will be a golden economic opportunity for the longer term. The obvious solution will be to urgently rebuild the world's destroyed forests, grasslands and rewilding agriculture land, to take it back to its original form before human farming so that it is inviting to native animal, bird and insect populations. Help Mother Nature help us. She moves fast with no political agenda. Australia's wide-open spaces can have additional valuable uses other than mining as carbon banks for the global market. I am sure our First Nations peoples can add more value here. Removing carbon dioxide from the atmosphere could reduce our planet's temperature to the levels seen prior to the Industrial Revolution. What a mission for Australia to lead the way in!

- Fully embrace and continue to back our innovators and inventors with an aim to avoid sending all our raw materials offshore (for others to process and gain the value added). The war against climate change will upturn the industrial landscape like never before, which will create massive opportunities for early movers. Let's continually reinforce that we are a 'thinking economy' and encourage, recognise and reward scientists and engineers to create new technologies, then support commercialisation of these ideas for new job creation and export value. We need to excite our young people more and let them let loose. For encouragement, just look at the international success of tech companies Atlassian and Canva. Get out of the way, baby boomers!

- Let's finally build a fast, green rail grid linking our major cities from the Gold Coast to Adelaide. It could travel the west side of the Great Divide and eventually to Perth, Alice Springs, and Darwin. Stop talking about it! Complementary government policy should then encourage the development of the linked regional towns and cities so that they lead our population growth, whilst slowing growth in Sydney and Melbourne. The pandemic has proven that populations are much better spread. Thanks to technology, small towns with lower housing costs are attractive, and should be encouraged to grow into medium-sized towns.

- Steel and concrete are part of our modern world, but they both produce greenhouse gases in their creative process. Let's develop green steel and green concrete/cement instead. Again, let's be one of the first movers and export these newly finished green products. We have all the raw materials in abundance.

- Be an active part of a global plastics solution, forcing manufacturers to migrate to readily and economically viable recycled/reusable products. We must rid ourselves of single-use plastics. Crazily, oil companies have diversified themselves into plastics companies – just another way to keep us addicted to carbon extraction industries. A world with less plastic, which does not add to

landfill or air pollution, will create new opportunities –
let's chase that possibility. New science is needed here.

OUR THREATS

- Not going forward as one with our First Nations peoples
  with a shared national vision reduces our potential for
  spiritual peace within ourselves and with each other.
- Obviously, doing nothing about climate change is like the
  frog in boiling water. Surely increased temperatures, flood
  and bushfires are alarm enough.
- Death of our oceans and coral reefs thanks to climate
  change, plastic pollution, overfishing, and chemical runoff.
  It's currently projected that by 2030, plastics in the
  world's oceans will weigh more than the fish stocks.
  Micro-plastics are already in the seafood chain, which
  means they end up in us as well.
- Economic reliance on China for both exports and import.
  We need to spread our eggs.
- Losing coal and gas jobs, while not building new industries
  to replace these. Unless we create new industries and
  jobs, we will effectively be moving jobs offshore. We need
  to wean ourselves off these industries in our own time,
  not a timetable forced upon us.
- Water supply and management – we need to continually
  improve the stewardship of our rivers and lakes. It is time

to reexamine our non-native agricultural pursuits like growing cotton and almonds (both of which heavily tax our water systems), and question if they have a sustainable future.

- Citizen political apathy. We need to force action in this decade. This is not a time for a 'she'll be right' attitude.

Chapter 3

Australia in the World Today

For the first time in history, mankind has an urgent, common global cause. There are 'clear and present dangers' to our ecosystem. Our human world, with its nearly 8 billion people, is overtaxing our ecosystem to such an extreme that we are not only causing life-ending climate change, but mass animal and plant extinctions. As a species, we all need to work together to bring a solution, to begin the 'grand repair' and get back in rhythm with the planet. Our indigenous people have a much better track record of living with their environment. Let's tap into their experience.

It was confirmed again at COP Glasgow 2022 that all developed countries must dramatically reduce carbon emissions by 2030, not 2040, if we are to have any hope of holding off the effects of climate change and keeping the planet at 1.5 degrees warmer than before the Industrial Revolution – a goal which is probably already beyond reality. We cannot stall and waffle on with these dates anymore. An accelerated emissions reduction is already needed, thanks to ongoing procrastination by governments and policymakers since the Paris Agreement. This, combined with a denial and deflection campaign by the carbon industries and their paid lobbyists, has stalled action.

As a responsible nation, we know that carbon extraction industries are pushing carbon dioxide and methane into the atmosphere, which is over-heating it. This atmospheric increased temperature then escalates the problem by causing the knock-on effect of –

- Melting the ice caps that are great reflectors of sunlight, and so adding more atmospheric heating.
- Heating of our oceans which try to absorb this extra sunlight, making them warmer and therefore melting more ice.
- Thawing the permafrost that awakens microbes which eat buried plant and animal material. This process releases carbon and methane, rather than keeping both greenhouse gases stored in the soil.
- Drying out forests, making them weak and hence more prone to bushfires and insect attack.

The Problem is Solvable

Globally we need to have total zero emissions by 2050. It can actually be achieved with progressive government policy driving the adoption of available green and clean technology. Economically viable solutions are absolutely available. Entrepreneurs are inventing cleaner industrial processes, greener power options and new electric transport options all the time. Engineering and science are responding to the challenge. Government policy is needed to encourage speedier adaption and adoption.

Luckily, the climate fight had some good news thanks to Trump's removal in the U.S. Now under Biden, America is becoming more focused on the herculean task of fighting climate change. At last, this means all major international players are onboard, which is vital for any chance of success. The big dogs must act, which includes us. The poor nations have not created climate change, but they will be the frontline victims. The developing world will be burdened with the environmental denigration and associated natural disasters (which are happening more often, and becoming progressively more severe). These countries do not have the resources to adapt, but we do. We must step up.

Yes, we are an island, but we share the oceans and the atmosphere. We cannot simply ignore these massive issues and think they will just go away, or that they are somebody else's problem. As they say, there is no Planet B – at least not for billions of people.

Australia will be gravely affected by climate change – more bushfires, more drought, more floods, more extreme temperatures and the resultant shrinking habitable area. If the 2019 Christmas bushfires were not a wake-up call, I do not know what would be. To add to their suffering, bushfire victims have to deal with the floods, made worse by the burned ground cover and more topsoil washed away. It was a real sign of things to come unless we act now.

All developed countries have a moral duty to act, but it is also in our self-interest to address climate change. The economic strength that gives us our enviable lifestyle is intertwined, and so endangered with the changing weather patterns. Solutions must be found and implemented urgently.

Greenhouse Gases

The global challenge is to halt the greenhouse gases being emitted into the atmosphere through industrial and agricultural processes and combustion engines by about 50 million tons a year.

Historically, using well-funded and focused corporate lobbying, carbon extraction industries have had a stranglehold on the energy supply and environmental agenda. Even with this entrenched, old-school political influence, energy markets are transitioning from carbon-based to sustainable green energy. In practical business terms, today solar and wind are very price-competitive and do not have the polluter's baggage for investors. Therefore, they are now being seen for what they are – a safer long-term investment.

The transition would be even faster if governments would end the coal, oil and gas subsidies to create an even playing field.

The downsizing process is starting to happen, with some large projects being canned in Alaska, Canada and China. In recent times, due to public and shareholder pressure, global banks are getting onboard and starting to remove their financial support for carbon extraction companies. Even China has stopped funding any new coal power stations in its Belt and Road Initiative. The tide is turning.

As a consequence, carbon extraction industries are doomed to become boutique industries, which has huge ramifications for Australia. I understand these industries continue to provide much income and many jobs, but they must be phased out. Let us start to influence the agenda by negotiating with our large national customers India, China and Japan, and agree on a realistic timetable for when the exports will stop as we all transition to green energy. No one expects any company to close its operation tomorrow. A phase-out period makes sense and is needed for all parties – the mining companies, their workers and our customers. People will need time to adjust on an agreed timetable. We should facilitate the process – not just wait until orders are no longer forthcoming. Our miners would then have a workable timeframe to transition their businesses, and so will the developing green energy providers in both Australia and offshore. I'm sure the miners will change their spots and diversify once the economic reality is made clear. Such a process would have a lot more surety than our farmers have year to year. They will adjust.

The previous Australian government's approval of the Adani mine is totally counterproductive to this global shift. It is against the trend and supports a dying industry. I understand that Queenslanders want jobs, but with its World Heritage Barrier Reef, Queensland will suffer some of the worst effects of global warming. Tourism dollars will be lost forever, affecting many more jobs than building a mine will, which will be mostly machine-driven.

If cared for (and that is a big if), the reef will last thousands of years, providing good, clean permanent jobs. How many years will a mine contribute, particularly in a world where people are walking away from coal? It is like building a horse-drawn carriage factory in 1920. Installing solar panels and batteries at every home will provide many more sustainable and well-paid jobs.

Protecting Our Oceans

As an island continent, the health of the world's oceans is clearly very important to our wellbeing mentally, physically and economically.

The oceans are suffering terribly from atmospheric heating, pollution, plastics along with rogue fishing fleets illegally venturing far outside their national waters and using super destructive drag net fishing, at times supported by their government subsidies. These out-of-control industries must be brought to account. It seems to me that policing these modern-day pirates could be a more productive role for the world navies, rather than sailing up and down the South China Sea. We must also support an increase in protected marine parks to help rebuild fish stocks without plastic in their guts!

Our Global Community

With these global challenges and opportunities, it is an appropriate time to reassess and to take a long-term view of how we want to participate in the global community, where we can add value, be supportive and be competitive. These are questions of principle, not just economic queries that need to be answered.

With the development and modernisation of Asia, the world has in fact moved closer to Australia during the last fifty years. The world has literally come to us. Our international neighbourhood continues to gain power and prestige. We certainly do not need to feel isolated and away from the main game as we once did, thanks to our colonial and European heritage.

Let's continue to engage fully and positively in the region. The lifestyle aspirations and desires of our Asian neighbours are continually increasing, which will create new demand for products and services. Let us be nimble and creative enough to react to these future opportunities. Our Asian neighbours have thrown off their colonial past, as we must. Unlike Britain, we do not have to join an Asian Union and give away a portion of our sovereignty to play.

The Information Age

The current Digital Information Age is forcing change much faster than the Industrial Revolution. We hear a lot about disruptive industries and products and the chaos they create whilst transforming communities. Maybe we need to place a few informed bets on which industries we are going to compete in, then be consistent and driven in our efforts as a nation. Put simply, what are we going to create and make for ourselves? What are we going to sell, and what are we going to buy?

In a global economy, scale/volume are becoming more and more important for many industries, but so is supply chain reliability. Focus is needed where we want to be self-reliant and competitive. Globalisation is not going away. That genie is out of the bottle, and will continue to make new technology and ideas available to all.

At the same time, the Information Age's tidal wave of progress cannot help but make some businesses, and therefore some jobs, obsolete. We need to recognise and accept this byproduct of global advancement and support those who are victims of this progress, not just stand on the sidelines while they struggle.

We need to understand that some of our citizens will be in the wrong place at the wrong time through no fault of their own. Some will be too old to retrain or relocate, but will need a lifeline.

These real human costs of progress need to be acknowledged and dealt with compassion and understanding in the 21st century.

A Global Citizen

Today Australia has a strong international image, mostly positive. However, our treatment of our Indigenous peoples, refugees and inaction on climate change is certainly tarnishing it.

With this in mind, do we feel the need to accept our responsibility to heal the rift with our First Nations peoples, and at the same time accept our role as a global citizen in the climate fight?

I believe there are some things we are not capable of as a nation, nor want to aspire to – for example, to be a global military force. But we can be:

1. United, strong and independent.
2. A better, more inclusive society for the Indigenous peoples of Australia.
3. A tolerant multi-cultural society (point number 2 must be tackled head-on for this to happen. There can be no exceptions.)
4. A good global citizen, contributing and working honestly to solve global problems.
5. A climate change champion, striving to become carbon neutral on a strict timetable.

6. A defender of the oceans. An environmental steward and leader setting an example to others.

7. A robust, competitive economy supported by our vibrant society, which encourages bold ideas and people 'having a go'. It's essential to take risks in order to bring about change. We must teach our kids that it is more important to try than to succeed. Real change can mean an ability to ignore the established systems to successfully create something new. If 'progress', as measured by the current society, is always the goal, it makes more sense to stay within that system – to play it safe at a time when we need more brave entrepreneurs in this fast-changing world.

8. A facilitator and mediator to people in conflict. I bet our First Nations peoples could add their experience here. They know firsthand what it is like to deal with deaf politicians.

9. A vibrant example of a democratic nation where citizens are able to lead a healthy, balanced way of life with a sense of real community and purpose. A nation where democracy works for all. The most multicultural democracy in the world.

10. A champion of the weak.

Chapter 4

Independence

Why should we bow to any offshore power? We are a confident, educated people who, I feel, should answer to no foreign power. We should not forfeit self-governing in any way, even ceremonially.

By declaring our independence now, as the people of our nation we have an opportunity to do something bold together – to right a wrong, to reconcile, to inspire, and to move forward as one.

We need to make a break from the UK and declare our independence. I believe this for five reasons:

1. IT'S TIME – it really is.
The Republican movement in our country has ebbed and flowed for decades, but to date has not succeeded in gathering the majority support needed to make the change.

Resistance from royalists has been strong. Many of our royalist politicians have thrown up many barriers against independence, desperately wanting to hang onto our colonial past like a security blanket. Their efforts reveal a lack of confidence in who we are as a nation and a people.

On the other hand, why don't we draw strength from the fact that the British public voted to leave the European Union, as they did not appreciate or want European influence on their own country? They believe they can manage their own affairs without offshore supervision. Now, as further encouragement, in the wake of Brexit, Scotland and Ireland are considering taking it a step further and pushing for their own independence, too. King Charles has his work to do keeping them united.

The Royal Family itself is in disarray (and some might say imploding, with Prince Harry leaving and Prince Andrew in disgrace, removed from royal duties). In this way, the royals aren't really ideal role models for our people. To be a working royal is a tough full-time job, and some have not measured up.

Having previously lived in London for six years, I understand firsthand that the Royal Family and its pageantry bring in millions of pounds to Britain through tourism. The Crown is a real focus and anchor point for many charities, which I applaud. But that is Britain, not Australia. We simply do not require British guidance or management anymore. I do not want to kick the Royal Family when they are down, but they need to concentrate on their own family issues and the UK domestic political scene. Let us thank them, wish them good luck and move on.

Timing could never be better. What more hints and encouragement do we need to take action?

2. WE ARE CAPABLE – most assuredly.

In day-to-day reality, we operate independently as a nation. So let us cut the umbilical cord. What are we afraid of? The move will be mostly symbolic. The Brits will still want to play against us in rugby, league and cricket, and any other game we choose, for that matter. It might even add more spice to any contest.

Since Brexit, the British government has been talking of renewing trading ties with the old Commonwealth countries, which is great. But let's do it as equals – both independent, proud countries learning from our past mistakes and acknowledging our history, but understanding our differences.

Does anyone seriously doubt that we can govern ourselves? I understand it may seem beyond us some days when our politicians open their mouths, but we can.

We should expect it of ourselves, demand it of ourselves.

3. A NATIONAL RESET/ UPDATE

The process of Independence in itself will be an opportunity for us to state who we are as a nation and who we want to be – to ourselves, and to the world. It will be a catalyst for self-examination and review.

It is not often that citizens have a real opportunity to take stock, reflect and fine-tune the course of their nation. Typically it happens after a war, a revolution or, maybe today, a pandemic. We can use an Independence Declaration to have a mini-revolution without firing a bullet or dropping a bomb.

4. RECONCILIATION WITH OUR FIRST NATIONS PEOPLES

Better late than never to remedy injustices. Such acknowledgement will allow us to move forward as one with Australia's Indigenous peoples. I believe it is impossible to truly reconcile with First Nations peoples without first breaking the tie with Britain, when you consider our Indigenous people never surrendered their sovereignty to the invaders. And so it would be an act of good faith and fairness to make this move, to show solidarity and empathy with the original custodians. We need to update who decides, who gets heard, and which stories get told, to tell the *whole* history of our continent.

As discussed in earlier chapters, climate change is real and mankind needs to urgently fix its relationship with nature and the animal kingdom. We thrive on clean air, pure water, a safe and healthy environment.

In this survival battle we are going to need all the help, all the experience and expertise we can muster, and not only from science and engineering. I feel the Indigenous peoples would really add knowledge to the climate challenge if we open our

hearts and minds. Time to invite ancient wisdom into the solution
mix.

5. TO RECOGNISE ALL OF OUR PEOPLE

Independence would reflect our nation's current cosmopolitan
makeup more accurately and honestly. We are not a British colony
anymore. We are Arrernte Australians, Italian Australians, Bunaba
Australians, Indian Australians, Wiradjuri Australians, Dharawal
Australians, Somali Australians, Aranda Australians, American
Australians, Bininj Australians, Irish Australians, Warlpiri
Australians, Greek Australians, Luritja Australians, Brazilian
Australians, Murawari Australians, Afghan Australians, South
African Australians, Gunggari Australians, Zimbabwean
Australians, Anindilyakwa Australians, Japanese Australians,
Chinese Australians, Vietnamese Australians...

We have a more colourful history than only the British
chapter. Today the only way to have a majority is to have a unified
group of minorities. We have that diversity in common with First
Nations peoples as they are many varied mobs with no one tribe
dominant.

As citizens, we all need to understand our pre-colonial history
a great deal better than most do today. That education must start
at school to raise natural curiosity amongst our children. We
should be encouraging the next generations to explore this. It will

drive understanding and acceptance of Australia's First Nations peoples on a broader scale.

As a nation, we have looked outwards a great deal – travelling the globe, seeing, experiencing, and learning about foreign countries and their customs, history, and culture. Our backpacking youth is world-renowned – mostly to Europe and now, since the '70s, to Asian countries as well. In fact, there are not many countries which are not on our itineraries these days (pre-Covid!).

Maybe it is time to look inwards more. There are 60,000 years of knowledge and wisdom we need to understand fully. Considering the history of the Greek and Roman Empires, along with the creation of Jerusalem, are relatively recent compared to that of the deep time of First Nations peoples, there is a wealth of knowledge of which we have only just scratched the surface.

The Lucky Country

Again, we are indeed a 'lucky country', at least for us white fellas. I think we now need to understand and genuinely accept this fact, and strive to ensure this gift is enjoyed by ALL, not just give it lip service. We cannot accept pockets of 'invisible people' being left out and ignored.

We all have a generational responsibility to leave a light footprint and pass on a better world to our kids. We most certainly do not need British guidance to do these things. The Brits definitely helped to build the Australia we see today and contributed to our great nation immensely, but now is the time to say thank you and move on. I am personally grateful for our larrikin attitude and sense of humour in 'taking the mickey', which I think is rooted in our convict past. I miss these characteristics living currently in the USA.

We all know the difference between right and wrong, easy and hard. Now we face a few hard decisions to do the right thing both domestically and internationally.

As an inspiring example, in recent times we have proven once again that bold visions and their execution are indeed a part of our core Australian DNA with the creation of the incredible NDIS. This is a generous, world-leading commitment that proves, as a community, we believe that no one should be left behind, alone or unsupported. It's a commitment by our nation that people with disabilities can have self-determination in their life plan – a plan devised with them, not for them. Other countries look at this undertaking with awe. As a man with a profoundly disabled daughter, I applaud Australia for this monumentally brave initiative.

The same generous and inclusive spirit must now be extended fully to the Indigenous peoples of Australia. It's time.

A Way Forward

So how do we make Independence happen? Now is not the time to be lazy or apathetic politically. If you are only going to give

politics real energy once in your life, I would say now is the time.
Our voices need to be heard by our politicians with selective
hearing.

Historically, often an obstacle thrown against an
Independence Referendum or simple plebiscite has been the
hurdle of deciding what sort of Republic we would want to be. For
example, perhaps we might opt for one similar to that of the USA,
with a popular elected President – or the French semi-presidential
model. Fundamentally this choice has been a politician's
smokescreen for inaction, dropping the referendum into the too-
hard basket. A classic example was during the last referendum on
Independence in 1999, when the Prime Minister of the day, John
Howard, gerrymandered the vote by adding a caveat that if the
people voted for independence, the PM would nominate the
President. With the justifiable distrust Australians have for their
politicians, he knew it would never get up with that condition. Sly
pollie – a true royalist.

The second popular stalling mechanism used by the
politicians is the habit of reminding us that we are a constitutional
monarchy, and that change would be expensive, time-consuming,
and create much debate. *It's not broken, so why change it?'* This
has been another tactic to deflect and postpone the independence
issue, to avoid action and maintain the status quo.

The Solution

I have a suggestion to keep it simple, keep administration costs
down, to correct the grave injustices and mistakes of our past, to
recognise the current multi-national makeup of our population,
and to provide a new solid progressive platform for our
independent future as a republic together.

Let's keep our constitutional monarchy, but change the
Monarch.

In response to the Uluru Statement from the Heart, why don't
we invite Australia's First Nations peoples to choose and provide
our Monarch from their ranks? They would decide who and how
the Monarch would be appointed and for how long. For example,
it could be an elder on a rotational basis, as voted for by First
Nations peoples every ten years. Clearly this is easier said than
done, as the First Nations peoples themselves are many different
people with many different languages, cultural practices and
different levels of integration. I, however, think they would
welcome such an opportunity. Dare we ask?

In declaring our independence, clearly we could simply go
with an elected Prime Minister, who could be sworn in by the
Chief Justice of the High Court – but we would miss a golden
opportunity to embrace our First Nations peoples and uplift our
national character. What better to way to recognise the traditional
owners of the land we all call home and to show respect for elders
past, present and emerging. The role would not be handed down

by birth, as is the case with the current royal family, but on merit. A Governor-General would not be needed, as the Monarch would be in-country – not 20,000 kilometres away. They could also change the title from 'Monarch', if they so decided. Something else might be more appropriate – say Elder, rather than President!

This would invite, and indeed encourage, the Indigenous voice in our future, just as they have requested in the Uluru Statement. It would make Australia's First Nations peoples more visible and unite us more as a nation, a whole nation.

I am sure such a changing of the guard would have challenges, and won't be some magic wand that solves the plight of our Indigenous peoples overnight. It would, however, be a step towards us getting to know them better – by listening to them to hear from them what is best for them, not us simply telling them our view and forcing our white opinion on them.

In 1867, the British political scientist Walter Bagehot published *The English Constitution* at a time when they were transitioning from an Absolute Monarchy with no parliament. He listed the three main political rights available to a Constitutional Monarch: *"The right to be consulted, the right to encourage, and the right to warn."* We could also add the 'right to be heard.'

Such an Australian Monarch would be a day-to-day positive influencer, not just a ceremonial figurehead sitting offshore. The role would add empathy, community thinking, and importantly patience to our political landscape.

The long-term health of our nation depends on our willingness to start listening to our Indigenous peoples and their tried and tested knowledge systems, which will hopefully contribute to them feeling treated respectfully and fairly.

The process to true equality could take another century, but unless we give it real energy, it will never happen. (Or should I say never never?)

The first appointed Monarch could start by heading the Makarrata Commission, to develop a treaty between the Commonwealth and Aboriginal people, lead the truth-telling, then recommend to government the necessary law changes to welcome and embrace First Nations peoples. (Makarrata comes from a word in the Yolngu language, meaning a coming together after a struggle, healing the divisions of the past, facing the facts of wrongs, to make things right and to living again in peace.)

At a time when the world is trying to tackle climate change, racism and inequality, what a bold step this would be to take together as a nation. What an example to the world and encouragement to other native peoples.

It's time to make the change, to let the truth-telling happen and the healing commence. We need to heal both our people and the land. Let us stand together on our own two feet as a proud independent nation with our own unique cultural identity, as unique as the island itself.

We should aspire to be an honest, trusted global citizen who has joined the fight against climate change and racism with our own house in order. Let us be a country that works for everybody.

LET THE DREAMING COMMENCE

Anyone under twelve, please continue to be a kid and enjoy it as long as you can. Growing up is a trap! Keep all the characteristics you were born with – your natural curiosity, your fairness, your laughter, your empathy, your kindness.

For all of us over twelve, find a place with a view where you can sit comfortably and open your mind. Then close your eyes and try to imagine the Australia you want for yourself, your kids, your grandkids...

Chapter 5

Constitutional Workshop 2024
(To Set the Stage)

Try to create your vision of what Australia should and could look like in 2050. I offer you mine...

- Australians voted in a landslide for Independence in 2023. The vote confirmed that the Monarch would be appointed by Australia's First Nations peoples.
- In late 2023 the first Monarch was appointed by a gathering of elders for a 10-year term. The Makarrata Commission was established with the Monarch as its head.
- A Constitutional Workshop (CW) was convened in 2024 with Indigenous, environmental, religious, business, sport, government, military, charity, union, industry, and political leadership present to:
  - outline our nation's values and goals for the 21st century,
  - recommend some legislature change for the Republic,

- facilitate the process and construct a
  timetable to Independence.

The workshop was hosted by the incoming Monarch and the support of the current Governor-General with the full backing of the King. The experience and counseling this brought to the table were invaluable. It was decided that these workshops would be hosted by the Monarch every ten years. Following this inaugural workshop:

- Independence was enacted on the 10th of October 2024.
  The date became the new Australia Day.
- The Northern Territory was granted statehood on the same
  day.
- New Zealand was offered statehood, but gracefully
  declined. (Joke, Joyce.)
- Some of the foundational decisions and changes to emerge
  from the Constitutional Workshop that have now been
  written into law – including:
  - Fixed-term for Federal Parliament of four years. There
    was a hope that the states would follow suit.
  - Party leadership (i.e. Prime Minister) could not be
    changed by the governing party for the first two years
    of elected term. In other words, the populace could
    expect that the party leader they elected would have
    at least two years to lead the nation and not be
    replaced by the party power brokers. Fixed terms

were deliberately designed to avoid snap elections
when the party in power thinks they are a good
chance to win and gain a few more years of governing.

- All electioneering to happen only in the month of
November of the election year, and actual election to
be held the first Saturday of December, with the new
government being sworn in January 1st. This allows us
citizens to enjoy Christmas and summer holidays
whilst the elected politicians go to work, getting ready
to govern.

▪ Core values adopted at the Constitutional Workshop:
  - Respect and appreciation for our land and our
    spiritual bond with it.
  - To live in harmony with nature.
  - Freedom for all, in all its aspects.
  - Clean air and pure water for all.
  - Zero tolerance of racism and sexism.
  - Affordable medical/dental care for all.
  - Affordable education for all.
  - Obtainable primary homeownership for all.
  - No-one left behind.
  - Compassionate attitude to refugees.

▪ The Monarch was charged with the ongoing safeguarding of
these values and that Government policy would reflect
them. These values sound simple and obvious, but they

were stated and publicly adopted to build a fairer and
more equitable society.

Other key insights to emerge from the workshop included:

- A National Museum and Cultural Centre celebrating the
  Australian Indigenous Peoples would be built in Canberra
  within the Australian Parliamentary grounds. It should be
  a peaceful memorial place to share knowledge and
  explore ideas. Its surrounding area would be rewilded. It
  would be charged with telling the truth of our history –
  both positive and negative – and educate those people
  interested on the indigenous lifestyle, including laws,
  family values, philosophy, medicines, foods, farming
  practices and land management.

- A general view was that the USA version of capitalistic
  democracy is not for us, where dog-eats-dog seems to
  prevail and a real class structure exists between the haves
  and have-nots, black and white, educated and
  uneducated. We Australians want and prefer a more
  community-based form of democracy, where a citizen's
  vote is more important than a corporation's. There was a
  desire to improve quality of life, not quantity of
  possessions.

- A decision was made to grant all our major rivers and
  waterways their own legal status, just as New Zealand has

granted legal personhood to the Whanganui River, then India quickly following with the Ganges and Yumana Rivers. This measure was designed to help and protect these natural resources against government and industry abuse in the future.

- A First Nations University would be established in Alice Springs, with specialties in land management; Indigenous culture and languages; solar, tide, and wind energy; native foods; and traditional medicines.

Chapter 6

THE YEAR 2050

Sitting in my garden, the air has cleared. Smog is a distant memory. The old noise of traffic is hard to detect, thanks to electric and hydrogen powered vehicles.

My local market is overflowing with fresh organic meat, seafood, vegetables and fruit – some from communal gardens, some from local schools, some from vertical and rooftop gardens. I grow some of my own.

Kangaroo has become our main red meat. Lamb and beef are more of a rarity. Native herbs and spices are a large part of the mix in my pantry.

Seafood is plentiful and sustainable. Lead, arsenic and plastic is all gone from their flesh and gut.

I count three First Nations peoples among my close friends. My great granddaughter learns the digeridoo and the Kaurna language at school.

My house, with its solar panels and green saltwater battery, is energy self-sufficient and carbon neutral. There are no power cables to be seen in my street.

We have one electric car, which has optional self-driving, and we often use public transport. Bike and skateboard lanes are everywhere. Sometimes I wish I was younger!

My wife and I now live in the granny flat we built in our backyard so my daughter and her family could have the family house. The easing of such planning codes have strengthened family units, lowered the cost of retirement, helped with housing stock needs, and also at times provided some-short term rental income for folk.

The grandkids and I visited the Great Barrier Reef, which is once again vibrant and healthy, as in my own childhood. Mother Nature has proven resilient given half a fighting chance.

We travelled by the fast train that links our great cities, with so many vibrant townships sprouting up along its route. Vast fields of solar panels and highlands sprinkled with wind turbines have now replaced all the fossil fuel-burning power stations to energise our green cities of today. It really was not a tough decision to choose slow-turning wind turbines over smoke-belching chimney stacks.

We had a day in Brisbane and ate in a pub without poker machines. The grandkids don't even know what they are, as they were banned ten years ago. Another indirect tax on the poor extinguished.

Tall native grasses move like waves from the wake of the train. Coastal and Great Divide forests look so big and strong. Their leaves have that healthy shine.

Last night I listened to our Elder deliver his annual catch-up. I recorded the speech, as experience has taught me that her messages can be quite subtle and I generally glean more from

them over a couple of listens. So I'll play it for you now...

Chapter 7

Elder's Address

"Tonight, as has become tradition, I will update you on the state of our Republic. Like many things in our great nation, my address has been given a nickname – 'The Elder's Report Card', which certainly brings a smile to my face. Maybe I should be wearing my old school blazer.

I am old enough to remember how Brexit, combined with the stress and lockdown of the Covid pandemic, was the catalyst for us, as a nation, to have a good look at ourselves. After that period of isolation from the world, we voted for independence and, not surprisingly, the world did not end. We still love to beat the Poms at cricket, and at anything else, for that matter. Very pleased that our test team is number one again.

In that good-natured spirit, wasn't it a wonderful moment last month when King William addressed our parliament and explained how, in his view, both our countries have been drawn closer since our respective nations voted for independence and self-rule? Kind of him to add that, towards the end of his address, that his grandmother, Queen Elizabeth, had confided in him before her death that she was surprised how long it had taken us to request independence and how glad she was when we finally did. Seems there were no hard feelings all around. It was time.

I thoroughly enjoyed William and Kate's company at the Rugby Test and the bottle of fine Scotch that was forthcoming from our little wager. Go the Wallabies!

It was a wonderful day when he officially opened the new library at our First Nations University which, as we all know, the Royal Family donated as a farewell gift.

Before I dive into the detailed report, I want to congratulate Professor John Mabeki of Adelaide Uni. Earlier today, I presented him with this year's Republic Medal for Civic Achievement for his work on eliminating ebola globally. Go Australia.

As per the norm for this annual address, I will touch on all the agreed report card subjects formulated at the Republic Workshop.

FIRSTLY, OUR REPUBLIC

We continue to punch above our weight on the world stage. I want to highlight a few of our achievements that we can be justifiably proud of.

You might recall that we were the sponsor and first signatory to the U.N. Managed Ocean Treaty of 2025. Since then, we have continually fought for the elimination of illegal over-fishing and been an active voice in building the global protected marine parks from around 3% to 35% of the world's oceans. To back our voice with action, we tripled our own protected areas from 2025-2035.

What an encouraging case study of global cooperation this has been – it really gives you faith that we can improve the world for our children. The ocean's fish stocks are back and thriving as a result. Let's hope they will never come under threat again.

As you are aware, my predecessor is now the U.N. Chief and has instilled a new level of trust, cooperation, and mediation amongst members. Her selflessness and calmness have been such a strength to the organisation, and she has proven to be a progressive agent of change.

I am interested to see that both Western Australia and South Australia are considering changing their names from the 'temporary' ones given to them by the British Army Corps of Engineers. I wish both states well on that endeavor. Perhaps eastern states might also look at their colonial names.

The Territory, as some old-timers still call it, has become a real destination for alternative lifestyle, with an influx of young people using its proximity to Asia as a springboard for their businesses. Some of these have sprung up from the First Nations University, and our greater awareness and acceptance of Indigenous medicine and land management techniques.

Moving along to OUR ENVIRONMENT – our AIR, WATER and ENERGY

Our game-changing carbon trading scheme, readopted after Independence, has started to be phased out and will be gone by

2060. This provides funds for new green tech startups, repurposing old mining towns, as well as retraining and relocating their workers. This was the economic catalyst for us closing our last coal power generation plant in 2035, and the total ban on our coal exports coming into force back in 2045. It successfully created a level playing field between the old carbon extraction industries and the green sustainable power industries. Hard economics prevailed, but the tax has now served its purpose.

In the last decade, as a nation we have again reduced our consumption of both water and electricity per head – this year by nearly 3%. We now rank third internationally. This has been a true national effort as we have all embraced new technologies, many of which were developed locally, and freely chose lifestyle changes for the greater good. Our water management skills have also developed export value. Location and climatically-appropriate agriculture is still evolving as we rewild some of our agricultural land and city greenbelts. Native birds are coming back, river fish stock is on the increase and actually safe to catch and eat!

In September we hosted the eighth global 'One Ocean Pact' conference. The Pact's core mission is to remove all the disused plastics from the ocean. This cleanup mission was greatly accelerated by several nations donating naval ships to the task force. It's wonderful that the 300 delegates were accommodated in the world's only underwater sustainable hotel and research centre on our Ningaloo Reef.

Net-Zero Energy

Today 85% of our residential housing stock is net-zero energy due to the large adoption of solar energy, saltwater battery tech (developed in Australia by a consortium led by the CSIRO), heat pumps and low energy consuming intelligent appliances. We have enjoyed an increase in community power broking, where families can donate their surplus solar generation to local charities. For example, now by the touch of an app, I can use my excess power to keep the light on at the local church or homeless shelter.

Back in July, the U.N. declared the hole in the ozone layer officially closed – such good news.

Our widespread adoption of free public transport has dramatically reduced the volume of cars using roads in our cities.

The Murray River mouth has been open and flowing for the last ten years, thanks mostly to the reduction of water being pumped out of it for irrigation. As we all understand, the Murray Darling River system, with its own legal identity, has a voice at the water rights negotiation table.

Smaller towns are growing and vibrant again as we continue to see a reversal of the Industrial Age migration to the big cities. Thanks to communication technology and improved intra-town/city transport, workers are not at any employment disadvantage when choosing to live in smaller cities and towns. In fact, the opposite is true as the reduced cost of housing and living

*means salaries can be more competitive. This helps to keep jobs
onshore.*

*Australia also has the planet's most geo-seismic stable
landmass. As good global citizens, you would remember that we
agreed back in 2028 to create the world's deepest deep earth
facility for storing used uranium. This project saw incredible
cooperation between Australia's First Nations peoples, the Federal
Government, the United Nations, and ten of the world's industrial
powers providing the technology and funding. All global nuclear
waste has now thankfully been placed at a depth that's harmless
to us or our environment.*

*Approved plastics in our society are now, by definition, fully
recyclable and will indeed be recycled (guaranteed by the
manufacturer), preventing any of it from getting into our
waterways and oceans. The chasing arrows logo now actually
means something. We have also reduced our use of plastics by
60% since 2025.*

Next I will talk about COMMUNITY

*The resurgence and proliferation of strong communities is
probably our greatest achievement: people being neighbourly,
people talking to each other. Respect for elders, and learning from
elders. By declaring independence, in my view, we gained more
confidence in our own identity, and grew more at peace with
ourselves.*

*We understand that the most important job most of us will
have is parenting. In that spirit, I am pleased to announce that the
number of stay-at-home dads continues to increase. The trend is
definitely that only one parent need leave home for work and it
can be either parent, not just automatically assumed it is the male,
as in the 20th century.*

*Used mindfully, technology has proven that more work can be
done from home, and research shows we have become more
disciplined in turning the smart machines off in the evenings and
on weekends. This has led to an improved life balance where we
can slow things down somewhat, and be more mindful and active
in our community.*

*Technology, including A.I., A.R., drones and robots, are now
working for humans, and we are not the addicted slaves to the
latest, greatest tech that we once were. We once feared for our
jobs with these modern technologies. What is clear now is that
they do give us more time for other activities. Fundamentally, this
has proven that all these new technologies drive costs down so, as
humans, we actually need less money to live a quality, happy
lifestyle. The old fear that robots were going to replace us all
seems to have gone away as we realise that robots can do the
mindless repetitive work, which, for humans, is mind-numbing and
unrewarding. This, in turn, allows us to work in more stimulating
roles.*

*Our track record shows that we use the extra free time
created by technology to put hours back into our communities. The
four day/ 32-hour working week has now been law for twelve
years – something that would not have been possible without the
automation provided by digital technology. I use that 'free' day to
do my jobs around the house and to shop, so that my weekends
are really about family and friends.*

*Community gardens are on the increase and proving to be
real social spots.*

*We have embraced the old-fashioned value that some lessons
must be taught around the family dining room table, not just by
school teachers. Kids are now encouraged to bring something they
cooked to show and tell. The trend where all family members learn
to cook something has slowed meal times down and strengthened
daily family communication and interaction.*

*Our classless sporting attitude seems to have really been
embraced by the broader society, where we now recognise that we
need all types and skills within our communities to make them
function successfully and to their fullest. As a result, I feel we are
showing more respect to each other.*

Now for EDUCATION
*As a nation, we hold dear our foundation tenant that low-cost
education and medical care are core rights.*

I am also feeling very proud that the First Nations history is now being taught in schools, starting in year 2 right through to University Masters courses.

The fact that a child can go from preschool to a university degree or a qualified trade for next to no cost is a real achievement and something we can be proud of as a nation. To see three of our universities ranked in the World's Top 50 was truly remarkable, and a tribute to the teams at each university and the tireless work and world-class research they do each year. What a resource for our children.

The push back in the 2020s and 30s for us to rediscover our skills of innovation and develop more hi-tech manufacturing led to the subsequent resurgence of cadetships and apprenticeships. These helped to develop trades – both traditional (electrician, carpenter, plumber) and contemporary (drone operator, vertical agriculture architect, robot controller, and hydrogen technician).

Many of our new technical colleges are based in the developing towns on the fast-track lines. This creates skilled workers where they are needed to build these towns.

The introduction of technical skill certificates/ diplomas of one-year duration has been widely adopted now by colleges and universities. We realised with technology changing so rapidly and new jobs being created continuously, we needed to fast-track the skills training for these new roles – we do not have the luxury of three to four years anymore to be internationally competitive. This has built real agility in our workforce.

Over 20% of public primary schools are now bilingual (mostly Mandarin, but a smattering of Japanese, French, and Italian as well), which is helping to improve the competitiveness of our workforce. In turn, it supports the base of our economic security – international trade.

An increase in music lesson availability in schools, thanks to new low-cost technology-based training and practice technologies, has also seen a real increase in the number of us who can play an instrument, which adds to our all-rounded lifestyle and supports mental health.

The push to get students walking to school again (even if it is from the nearest bus or train stop) to encourage independence and self-sufficiency seems to be working, and has improved traffic around schools as the number of chauffeur mums and dads is in decline.

Thanks to the ever-expanding older buddy network, school bullying is now a real exception, not the norm, but we must always be vigilant on this issue. Many of our professional sports stars have donated their time to this project.

The last two decades have proven that competition is fine and medals for winners are fine, preparing kids for the real and very competitive world.

*Great to see the number of fruit trees that have been planted
at schools and universities, and maintained by students!*

*More and more schools are building citizen gyms, which are
available after school hours and on weekends for locals. This has
proven a great source of income, as some gyms allow membership
to be paid for with volunteer hours.*

Now for HEALTHCARE, including the NDIS

*NDIS continues to be the world-leading disability program and
global benchmark. We hosted the World Disability conference last
July, where I was honoured to be the keynote speaker. Our
expertise is being sought actively by other nations and has
spawned a new knowledge-export industry.*

*Following the successful introduction and establishment of
the NDIS, our 'people seeing people' campaign (first introduced
twenty years ago) continues to be a success, where everyday
Australians are encouraged to just say 'G'day' to the disabled
members of our community and their carers. This small, easy and
free gesture has helped the assimilation of the disabled into our
community, and really shown the carers that they are valued and
respected. Life can be lonely for both the disabled person and the
carer. Gone are the days where our disabled either lived in poverty,
locked away in institutions, or living with exhausted parents,
siblings or children.*

This acceptance in creating a more disability-aware community has had an unexpected benefit in that it has helped with mental health. People with depression come forward and talk about it a lot more, therefore reducing the stigma of any disability and subsequent treatment.

It is hard to imagine that loneliness even exists in a society that seems so welcoming and laid back, but it has and still does. We have made great progress with institutions like Men's Sheds and the volunteer retiree program at primary schools, but we can always do more to open up to neighbours, work colleagues, etc. We as individuals must always be open, thoughtful and compassionate, which takes effort, but the rewards are mighty.

Diet

The anti-sugar campaigns of the 2030s are now really starting to show long-term benefits, with diabetes down by 40% and obesity rates the lowest for fifty years. I am simply amazed each time I visit a supermarket at how the product mix has changed so dramatically in the last thirty years – more fresh food, more self-packaging, more herbs grown on-site, etc. My local store has cooking lessons after hours, which follow on from the school's basic cooking program.

Community and school gardens have fostered an increase in general knowledge of our environment and what is good and natural for our bodies. Getting our hands in the dirt is a real day-to-day therapy as well.

Our four super-size medical centres, strategically placed in Brisbane, Darwin, Perth and Cairns as an economic boost to our cities close to Asia, are providing much-needed healthcare and recovery services to both locals and an international clientele. This medical tourism provides funds for more research and makes the centres more financially sustainable.

Medicine and Drugs

Remember smoking? What a thing of the past. Just seems so old-fashioned now.

I have observed with interest the assimilation of marijuana and mushrooms into our society, due mostly to millennial and Gen X acceptance. It's now available in teas and sweets, and is basically treated with care, like alcohol. This has allowed our police forces and courts to concentrate on eliminating hard drugs. As an aside, aren't the Customs robots amazing? They are proving to be a helpful extra tool at airports, where they can detect all sorts of drugs being carried on passengers.

Medical research is still a great industry for the nation, creating many support businesses and employment. I am heartened to know many Indigenous medicines and healing practices are now in mainstream practice.

Technology gains have reduced the cost of medical services greatly and allowed the elderly to stay in their homes longer. We can now scan a suspected skin spot with your phone, and text it to a centre for evaluation. Simply amazing.

Our ARMED FORCES

Our military, although small on a global basis, is one of the most professional and agile in the world. It is resourced with the latest equipment and the people are as well-trained as any developed country.

The three Special Forces bases of Perth, Darwin and Townsville are all now fully operational to increase our quick response capabilities.

Our expanded Commando and SAS forces continue to protect the villagers in two African nations by providing safe havens in a number of conflict areas. I am hopeful that sub-Saharan Africa is close to peace. Amazing how the developed world's eyes turned to the region as the Middle East lost its political muscle thanks to the decline of the oil industry.

With the new unmanned technologies available, we have been able to do more with our relatively small force – the classic example being the international water fence we have built off of our North and West coast. Here beacons/satellites and unmanned patrol boats can monitor all traffic, and can tell the difference between a whale and a boat. This is like a modern-day version of our forefathers netting Sydney's beaches for sharks.

Our strategic policy of buying USA weapons has simplified the supply lines and allows for a quick ramp-up of equipment when needed, while also supporting the USA base presence in Darwin, Broome and Gladstone.

The gap year program introduced by the military forty odd years ago continues to be an overwhelming success, where students completing high school can train one full year within the services to increase our military preparedness. It's wonderful that such volunteers are then allowed to complete their university or college education for free. I do want to add that as the Gap Year Soldier numbers have swelled, there has been a real increase in the general population's awareness of the real value of our military.

These younger ranks have also heralded a resurgence in the RSL clubs, where membership is booming and associated youth clubs are once again thriving. The RSLs are also providing true welcome mats for returned soldiers, where they can obtain support and just have a real chat with like-minded Australians – invaluable to their own recovery.

Let's turn now to HOUSING and INFRASTRUCTURE

The world's largest wind turbines on Port Phillip Bay provide 20% of Melbourne's energy needs and some rather large sailing marks! They are so silent that the No.3 turbine now has a man-made island supporting a restaurant and bar attached to its legs at water level. The associated symbiotic battery storage has proven a real win as grid stability is now high in all conditions.

Commercial rocket planes are a reality now, as developed in a public-private partnership with the diversified BHP, SpaceX, and Boeing. Their adoption now means New York and London are only ten hours away.

With the completion of the latest project to increase the Snowy Mountain Authority (SMA) hydro capacity it now supplies 80% of Canberra's power.

Transport

The final leg of the fast train to Perth was completed this year, now linking Brisbane, Gold Coast, Sydney, Canberra, Melbourne and Adelaide. Darwin from Adelaide is near completion.

50% of the nation's car and truck fleets are now driverless, and our truck, train and car fleets are now all-electric. Car ownership per household has reduced on average from 2.5 in 2020 to 1.75 as transport sharing services are adopted. I strongly agreed with the freight companies deciding that, even though it was possible, rural deliveries will still be with drivers as there is a community social benefit.

Tourism

With our nation's natural beauty and our multiculturism tourism will always play a big part in our economy. I have enjoyed one of our latest attractions – the tour ferries on the Darling River, thanks to stronger water flow, which has brought tourism to previous remote towns. Slow ferries are now linking Newcastle and Wollongong to Sydney, Geelong to Melbourne, and Freemantle to Perth. Not everything has to be fast. If you want speed, catch the train.

The rural zoning legislation that allows farmers to allocate up to ten one-acre lots for cabins on their properties (for weekenders and retirement living) has brought the city and country closer, as well as supporting decentralisation. It really is wonderful to have a small cabin on a working farm, where you are surrounded by nature and agriculture with someone else looking after it! The part-time city transplants have brought business to local towns and helped make them more vibrant. My own 'host farmer' now has a number of city mates, who put him up when he's in town. I also know he gets quite a lot of volunteer hours of work out of the 'squatters' at harvest time or round-up, followed by meals together – what fun!

SPORT

Such a big part of our culture and way of life. We are still one of the most sport-mad societies in the world. I think a key reason for

this is that it is probably our leading way to decompress and has
proven to be a real cultural melting pot. The last thirty years have
seen a steady increase in participation at all ages, which has
definitely helped to reduce obesity levels. As much as we
appreciate watching our international sporting stars, we can have
fun and enjoy playing ourselves, whatever the level.

The establishment of a sports lottery by the Federal
Government in 2024 has seen a real increase in funding for the
amateur and minority sports. This in turn has seen a resurgence of
our Olympic team's medal haul.

Boot camps seem a way of life now and have become a
tourism business in themselves. Endurance and survival sports
continue to be an offshoot of these camps.

Wheelchair basketball by able-bodied folk has really helped us
all to understand the challenges of people with disabilities, in turn
building a more inclusive society.

IMMIGRATION

Like most nations, we have two general types of immigration –
those who choose to come freely through mainstream application
channels, and refugees who have relocation forced upon them. We
recognised that both groups add skills and culture to our
workforce. They have added colour and texture to the fabric of our
nation.

*Clearly, refugees have complex histories and suffer
tremendous stress due to relocation, along with causing angst, at
times, in our own communities.*

*We have consciously chosen to support the U.N. Refugee
Agency's global programs to help these desperate souls resettle
and to start again. 'To start again' – easy to write, quite another
thing to do. Put yourself in their shoes (or lack of) for just a
moment. Imagine, after finishing your education and working hard
to get your own home and start a family, then having someone
take it all away at gunpoint. Or never getting a chance of
education, due to your gender or social status. Then imagine how
good an outstretched helping hand and a smile would be in those
dark days. It might be just enough to help brush yourself off and
start again.*

*Even though it was hugely controversial at the time, when the
decision was made to move the refugee processing centres onto
the mainland, it was a game-changing moment. This was done by
utilising existing military bases with their proximity to towns,
services, and experts who were readily available to accelerate
processing and help with transitional skills for successful
applicants. While their applications are processed, we now have
work available – both on-base and off, which has bolstered self-
esteem, helped restore pride, and accelerated the healing process
for the folk who are generally traumatised by the forced change.*

English classes, with a sprinkle of Aussie humour, are held in the evenings for adults.

In addition, local volunteer groups are now:

- *Introducing refugees to Aussie sports – cricket, footy etc using the base facilities. It's now also possible to attend a local club match.*
- *Hosting barbeques.*
- *Helping to set up community gardens.*
- *Organising fitness groups.*
- *Conducting classes in Australian history and geography.*

The result is that our refugee management system is now a world model used by many nations. This is held up as the gold standard by the International Refugee Commission, as opposed to the embarrassment it once was for our nation. Some of these new Australians have even joined our military.

It seems like the old-fashioned cricket ball has become the new worry bead for some of the new Australians, as I see them during my visits spinning the ball in their hands and juggling them around. Who would have guessed?

Every refugee now receives their team supporter's pack when their resident status is granted and they head off to their new home.

As a nation, we have welcomed many Pacific Islanders in recent times, as part of our neighbourly duty. Thanks to global warming, their own homelands are shrinking and, with it, their economic viability. Sadly, the global environmental efforts were not soon enough for these folk. If we ever need a reminder that we are one planet interconnected, just take a look at how islanders were devastated by centuries of industrial gases being pumped into the atmosphere by the developed nations. Hopefully, with the current progress being made, they may be able to return one day.

I am always amazed when I chat to the firstborn generation of immigrants to hear how they already sound and act so Aussie. As a nation, we have managed to absorb great things from the immigrant cultures, but at the same time, our core DNA as Australians seems to have gotten stronger through this assimilation process. I guess it confirms people want to be Australians first, whilst still recognising their roots.

The purity of our environment and our general community-based lifestyle is proving a real attraction to overseas folk. It seems old-fashioned values of honesty, fairness, straight-talking, humour and compassion are being appreciated all over again.

ELDERS and RETIREMENT

Life expectancy is now around ninety-five years – which is quite incredible really, thanks mostly to some medical breakthroughs in the early detection and prevention of Alzheimer's and dementia. With this increased life expectancy, retirement age is now seventy.

My people believe that society is healthier if you keep generations mixed together in the community, without hiding our elders away. Since adopting the Indigenous way of trying to avoid sending elders to a nursing home, more elders are staying in their homes and staying in their communities. This allows a tremendous wealth of knowledge to be passed on. I hope my kids are paying attention to this point!

Well, that is it for me. Thanks for listening and thanks Australia for another fine year in our maturity as an independent republic.

In closing, I want to remind us of what Nelson Mandela said on arrival in Australia:

'You can smell the peace and taste the freedom.'

Thank you."

From the Author:

*I want to wish my daughter, Alexandra, good luck in her quest
to understand our First Nations peoples history and culture
and her project to draw out their wisdom.*

CPSIA information can be obtained
at www.ICGtesting.com
Printed in the USA
BVHW050740030123
655320BV00015B/1491